Not in Heaven

Not in Heaven

Molly Minturn

SOUTHWORDeditions

First published in 2018
by Southword Editions
The Munster Literature Centre
Frank O'Connor House, 84 Douglas Street
Cork, Ireland

Set in Centaur 11pt
Printed by City Print, Cork, Ireland

ISBN 978-1-905002-54-2

Contents

For Beatrix Wolfe

Amor Fati

So I've done it now
I am the girl alone in the woods.

The horse ran away
and I didn't cry.

I can play Beethoven loud as I want,
mournful Beethoven to deaf trees.

I like the way
his music goes back on its word.

My own cruelty makes the trees grow
crooked and spindly, little witches;

they lean away from me
like the oboes at the top of the score.

O, they say to the higher plane,
away from me. A dream

can take the shape of a life—
bees push themselves soundlessly

deep within white petals.
The great house and missed chance

and your face at the end of the hall
saying *be good, be good,* without

saying anything at all.

DECADENCE

The new gold rush
is on in Greenland—

our fate is floating
among the broken

ice caps, failed
meringues. Leave

the window open
all night, when the sky

could be the open sea
for all we care. There

is no sun today, but
my daughter pulls

herself onto my bed
to tell me about the storm.

I have just been dreaming
of her—the two of us

smoking angel dust
in a European thrift shop.

How beautiful she was
in a world without

windows, just a yellow dress
floating up to the ceiling.

Triptych

My father had his own room
in our old house in Manchester,
cramped between the master
bedroom and the children's hallway.
He built skylights into the ceiling
because the house faced north
and we needed all the light
we could get.

In the afternoons, long before
he came home from Boston
I waited for him,
lay on warm patches of rug
where skylights hit, sketched
my hand on scraps of used
tracing paper, rejected architecture,
pulled his tortoiseshell shoehorn
out of the closet and fit
the smooth scoop of it against
my palm. My mother watched

me from his bureau, three of her,
a triptych in a red frame—the only
bright thing in the whole room:
my mother at age seven on a camel
in Egypt, eighteen in Sweden,
twenty-nine, heavy with me inside.
I liked her there; contained in red.
She didn't talk to the shoehorn, or to me.
I liked all of us there together, the whole
family, just before evening came on.

A Child's Garden of Verses

The stairway is blue, hums the hour. Very close,
the smell of plastic forsythia. I've been ruthless
in the basement and come away with Uncle's shooting cape
and the game we called Blockhead. Preoccupied with doves—
the way their necks wretch when they fall. Green
cape, swoop, the orderly descent. It makes me
woozy for all-school chorus, the timbre,
the brunette altos. Repeat the word *cadence*
until something awful. This room—
frosted bedspread and Latin diploma. I have taken
a shine to Grandfather's neckties and baby ring.
I pocket the funeral, the silver from the converted piano.
Outside, our meadow of creamed corn. Please
turn me deciduous. Scarlet the parlor.
My terrible arms wing up in the dark.

LADY

My brother couldn't wait to be a nun,
pulling his pastel baby blanket into a habit.
Mornings spent kneeling in the sun
with the fleas. Suffering is for the faithful.

I played dress-up to become foreign,
—a hat from a real funeral,
the little black veil let me see as the adults do.
Ladies are the opposite of mothers, hidden

but bright. Like watching communion
from the last pew, a silver glint—
The way they must love, behind shades.
Some mornings I joined him on the porch,

in the far corner near the tennis rackets.
Our burnt heads, unanswered, debtless.

WAKE

Open your bedroom window in the heart of winter.
Wrap the wool blanket around you, the one
your brother once used to pin you beneath

for hours, held down by the chesterfield
and an ottoman. You resisted until
you were underwater, your eyes and lungs

filled with light, and you went to sleep
on the carpet. When you stopped struggling
you were left alone. Alone now, let the night

air in. The snap of it in your lungs like croup,
your mother rocking you in the bathroom, the tub
filled with steaming water, how she sang your name

again and again as if to call you back. Listen now
to the buzzing of electric wires outside
your window, the constant murmur, the way

you imagine the world must work—the secrets
people keep and then tell. It must be like waking
to a room full of yellow roses, knowing those truths.

Bouquet after bouquet from friends—they did not
forget you after all. Like waking to her humming
in a steaming room, life coming back to your lungs.

Lo-Fi

You died just before the world became immediate.
You were ready for it—bought your phone and tablet,

sat me down to talk about the doomed future of print.
I shook my head. We made plans for the apocalypse.

If only I could capture you through Instagram,
show you the nostalgia for a dead age;

I'd choose the most mournful filter.
You should see how people are everywhere

and nowhere now. What does it mean
to have a profile? Ghost fingerprints,

a little wailing wall. So you took your life amid
some scraggly trees on a morning

with its heart burned out. Why
shouldn't I still wait for your call?

Rust

I like the idea of time being flat, that somehow I am sitting in this
chair right now and also riding in a car-seat in the back of the Peugeot,
examining my mother's head over the seat, the river of her new perm.
When I walk alone through the neighborhood and feel like I am on a
sound-stage, or beneath an enormous bell jar, there is meaning in that.
The thought that I have died a thousand times and wind back up in
the same place, circling around the same people, doesn't frighten me
at all. Certain people are like books I have read before but don't quite
remember. Perhaps we all played sardines as children and were pressed
together underneath a bed, then parted quickly to find our mothers.
When my daughter was born I looked at her face and said *yes, of course.*
The other day I made pancakes for just the two of us. She sat watching
me and when my back was turned I felt her adult presence in her chair,
like a quickening. I served them up as I have so many times before—
golden, flat circles.

Bridge

Rust and old wives' tales, Ohio—
though I've never traveled there.

Criss-cross of beam support
and birds flying in an arc right through it,

a slow French film.
Bamboo leaning sideways, not from wind

but groundswell. People drive by below,
on the highway, merging. It felt right—

I am frightened
to speak in front of crowds,

or even at a table in the evening
with friends, as they lean closer to listen,

forks paused, as if
I am a good storyteller. In my mind,

I see puppets from a children's show,
how easy it must be in felt clothing,

visiting one another in treehouses
to work out little conundrums.

The answers often come from song. Some are timid
but they still know what to say.

I am always thinking of leaving
the way the stealthy do, quietly

through a tunnel beneath the scenery.
It is not a railroad bridge at all, but the peak

of a college stadium—a place to fill with noise and light.
I made a mistake; it wasn't remarkable.

Foxglove

As often as I revisit
the park in the middle

of the country soft
in the center of my brain

I cannot remember
the entrance or streets

beyond, only the fields
spread flat as sheets

and the hollow in the trees,
like standing in a clavicle.

And time is a heartless
thing, a thin gold chain

that leaves a rash.
The wind skimmed

the meadow, your skin
and then was shelved.

T̲here is L̲ost. T̲o T̲his

In memory of happier times,
our fall print issue comes up again and again—
we never have leftovers and I don't get dead.

The best editor I've ever worked for
(this is a Les Misérables person of all time).
Our fall print and holding up running again.

Yes, it's coming soon, both in print and spooky:
future of journalism, and all day.
There is a plane crash in Merriam-Webster.

Here is a funny joke now.
The best film about my friend Kevin's memorial service will be here!
You, guys, I am such good care of a headline. Ha ha.

The best editor I've ever hope for
quiet in the story of this.
You, guys, I am unable to clarify.

Our fall print issue will try again soon…
Lots of working hard today, I have I mentioned that I am very sad.
I was like the heap of myself.

So very sorry I am such a hot piece tonight.
This is in a haunted ring.
I was just cried at the dawn of the center of this

All the quiet poets
just cried sending love to see one.
Very happy to my life is as sad when you are.

This is how our ending goes, let the old
time for now, I'm going to stop talking/ commenting on fire—
this is damn good editors are.

This is great distances to reach me.

Winter Troika

I'm never quite ready for it.

Sunday now, here, eating grapefruit with a tricky little spoon while outside
  the gloaming.

The cars tight and packed like ice on teeth and way off the bald hills never
  change.

Why do I bother with the window or the hour?

Now someone else is looking, too, out on his deck across the way, wind
  quilting his hair.

He is so still and I want to pull him apart like a matryoshka doll and meet
  his other self.

I know there will be a bright rose lacquered on his chest and a stitched
  yellow bonnet like Easter.

He is still out in the air, gaunt as Lincoln.

How did we arrive here?

Always the purple smeared sky, always the dormant garden.

My face hot on the pane, too dark to see much anymore, but something
  apart from me still humming, gold-leafed.

The Natural Order

We were taught that certain types of moss were prehistoric trees shrunk
down over centuries.

She led us through the woods after school on Wednesdays as we clutched
compasses and pH strips.

This fungus will consume you over time if you slip into it, our instructor said.

Her blonde hair held back in a scarf, nothing like our mothers.

Two hawks overhead, a fallen striped maple tree.

In my pocket, a half graham cracker with peanut butter.

This was the world; a boy far ahead of me in the wide cold, the smudge of
his red fleece, the way someone looks underwater in the deep end.

If you see an owl in the daylight, chances are it's rabid.

On my thumb, a thin scar, pale as a weak flashlight, from my brother
slicing through with a can of cheese balls.

That day had been hot and we'd worn swimsuits in the garden.

Things easily identifiable—zucchini, cantaloupe, my thumb under the
spigot, the back deck resplendent in the middle of July. Tiki torches.
Aluminum chairs.

Two crushed beetles spread across the planks.

But here the forest opened into more of itself, and I was hungry. We
paused by a reddening stream.

In two days, these waters have journeyed all the way from the Arctic.

We noted this down and the stars began lumping together above.

In my pocket, a thick mass of crumbs.

The Copper Age

The oldest crown in the world
is a black metal ring
topped with vultures and doors—
a miniature model of a sky burial.
The oldest crown in the world
is a relic from the Copper Age,
and doesn't that sound
almost as beautiful as a coiled
bracelet on a smooth arm?
Study the long table of prehistory
and you are wearing
the oldest crown in the world.
One vulture pecks at your hair,
the other looks to the sky,
the doors hover beside each temple,
and your mind becomes a ceremony.
Every dream you've ever had ends
in a bleached cave above the Dead Sea.

Bachelor in Paradise

I wonder where you go
in the seven hours of surgery

when they illuminate your body
radiate your the spine

This time it's an aneurysm
in your right leg, little huffhead

Where are you
when they put you under?

Let's say death is just a thing, no
different from shutting the closet door

and leaving you afraid
among your mother's shoes

Let's say it leads to something new
and inconceivable, an island

beyond the island
you knew off the coast of Maine

where the green tent is waiting
on a quilt of pine needles

Your veins are full of it now
saltwater and empty, northern air

and the sleeping bag's flannel
says *here you are, boy.* You built a fire

for yourself without trying
and soon it is inside your throat

all the words you could not speak
specks of ash now, coughed out—

October Recess

Running down the hill,
we are Indians and ponies.
Hundreds of jackets
hum color in dark weather
amid the smell of milkweed.

Inside of my mouth
a loose tooth slips back and forth.
I chase Annabel
and feel the tight gum thread snap.
Secret taste, red as the leaves.

I press the new hole.
Light flashes behind my eyes.
I see my father
as an old man, our house gone.
This is the start of my death.

I pull my daughter in her green wagon through the neighborhood. The wind blows and I feel alive.

I turn around to remark on the mountains through the trees. *Forward!* she says before I have opened my mouth.

According to Schopenhauer, human will is futile and causes great pain. The only way to escape is by negating all desires.

Schopenhauer also hated his mother.

I have painted my bedroom a sea foam shade for a "calming effect."

On waking in the mornings, I like to pretend I am somewhere above the earth though not in heaven.

Schopenhauer might call this "aesthetic contemplation."

I've never really understood metaphysics.

In that green room, though, I float in a glass bottle like a model of a ship.

I remember the dream I've just left, of my old flame climbing out the window and the great pain.

I love you! I say out loud to the ceiling.

Pilgrim

In my early teens I was an acolyte
at the Episcopal church the next town over.
I want you to see me in the vestry, snapping
up my red gown and pulling the billowing white
blouse over my head. I want you to see
me walking up the aisles holding the golden
crucifix in my gloved hands, the stick
above my knees. The light glinted on the cross,
the minister blessed the wafers and wine and I believed
none of it. But sitting in my private pew I breathed
in the scent of burning candles and holy oil,
and felt myself step out of my body. It was you—
I sensed you from many years away; in my little
wooden box I was no longer lonely. All of this is to say
I will not let you go unless you bless me.

THE BOOK OF COMMON PRAYER

Turn on every light in the house.
Open each door, your life
an advent calendar

where we can all be free, quietly.
That late-night prank at summer camp,
a canoe on the dark lake, underwear

woven into a quilt, covering the raft.
In the morning let it remain, fluttering
lace and hearts, encircled by water

and pines. Behind each door
your father, a baby in an incubator, fists
startling against his face, white peonies.

Your brother in a newspaper crown,
standing on the king-size bed,
his bloody lip, his eyes closed,

listening to the dead. Strings
of light around the birdbath
all through the winter. Your mother

at the window waiting for the sparrows.
She does not turn around. The sorrow
of her shoulders framed in the window.

Speak her name and she will return.

orning. I walk to the Mighty Mart, sun stuck in my thorax. The Mighty
art is so far away. I'm not going to give up.

y wool coat is like England and walled-off gardens and war children. Dank
in, no butter.

meone passes me in a car and waves. I don't think I know her but maybe we
re friends once.

usual, the trees look furious.

e stream has caught a plastic bag, blue and smeared. Once someone carried
towards home. Do people just open their windows and release bags to the
iverse? For a long time I thought love was the answer but now I think it must
bags.

ck at home with my waxy tub of milk. I sit in the study with the milk on my
ees.

an't go into the kitchen. The light in the kitchen is too glittery, like jazz
nce. It is morning—the light should be calm as small birds.

meone is in there, very still in the corner with the pale china.

e problem is that it's my other self and she doesn't know I'm here. She has
eyes and I don't want to see them.

ow she's running water and humming, flexing her calves. I hear toes clicking.

now just how the water feels on her hands.

small, unremarkable burn.

THE RAFT

We are led by our mothers
through the water,
some of us in wings.
Our teeth snap from the cold
and if we are sorry
for anything in our lives
now is the time
to spill it.
Our raft is only wood
and rope, though far below
our dangling feet, dark stars
from another universe.
If we are sorry,
its ladder will take us
directly to the sun.

Autobiography

Masconomo Park, I live in you.
Won't you please reveal yourself.
I know you are here—
cedar and gazebo,
the dead-boy marsh, all purple,
and the ghost carnival—
funnel bread, Gravitron, Scrambler.
Let the harbor freeze.
Let's skate carefully downstream.
Winter life—heather and rockrose.
Is it far to sea?
How often do you think of me?
Honestly, I have no skates
and I don't know how.
I will wait at the banks in my duck shoes.
Please do not fail me.
My heart is a quail.
Little town of burning light,
palm-sized birds and hobby horse.
Winter does not end.
I am here by the water, my last day on Earth.
Wind in my hair and everything.
My dusk familiar
like an old recording,
reedy and unmistakable.

Acknowledgements

"Decadence" and "There is Lost. To This" appeared in the *Iowa Review*.
"Wake" appeared in *Boston Review* and *Poetry Daily*.
"The Book of Common Prayer" appeared in the *Alabama Literary Review*.
"A Child's Garden of Verses" and "Midwest" appeared in *Bennington Review*
"Autobiography" and "Pilgrim" appeared in *Sycamore Review*
"Amor Fati" appeared in the *Iowa Review's* online Poetry Month series

"Rust" was influenced by the television show *True Detective*.

Thank you to the poetry faculty at the University of Virginia and the
Iowa Writers' Workshop, especially Lisa Russ Spaar, Charles Wright, and
Rita Dove; my friends Megan Fishmann Getten, Emma Rathbone, Wendy
Glosband, Lindsay Graham Robinson, Aaron Carico, Judy Le and Jack
Hamilton; and my family—Suzanne Freeman, Richard Minturn, Brendan
Wolfe, Jake Minturn, and Ray Szwabowski.